Options Trading for Beginners

The Ultimate Guide to Mastering Options Trading and Stock Trading in 45 Minutes or Less!

Copyright © 2015

All rights reserved. No part of this book may be reproduced in any form without permission in writing from the author. Reviewers may quote brief passages in reviews.

Disclaimer

No part of this publication may be reproduced or transmitted in any form or by any means, mechanical or electronic, including photocopying or recording, or by any information storage and retrieval system, or transmitted by email without permission in writing from the publisher.

While all attempts and efforts have been made to verify the information held within this publication, neither the author nor the publisher assumes any responsibility for errors, omissions, or opposing interpretations of the content herein.

This book is for entertainment purposes only. The views expressed are those of the author alone, and should not be taken as expert instruction or commands. The reader of this book is responsible for his or her own actions when it comes to reading the book.

Adherence to all applicable laws and regulations, including international, federal, state, and local governing professional licensing, business practices, advertising, and all other aspects of doing business in the US, Canada, or any other jurisdiction is the sole responsibility of the purchaser or reader.

Neither the author nor the publisher assumes any responsibility or liability whatsoever on the behalf of the purchaser or reader of these materials.

Any received slight of any individual or organization is purely unintentional.

Table of Contents

Introduction

Chapter 1 - What is Options

Chapter 2- Why Trade Options

Chapter 3- What You Need To Know

Chapter 4- A Few Words Of Advice

Chapter 5- Options Trading Strategies

Conclusion

Introduction

First and foremost I want to thank you for downloading the book, Options Trading for Beginners

The Ultimate Guide to Mastering Options Trading and Stock Trading in 45 Minutes or Less!

In this book you will learn how to understand options trading and learn how you can use options trading to create an additional income stream. You will learn exactly what options trading is and how you can use it to benefit you.

You will learn how you can use options trading to reduce the risk of losing money in the market and to help you earn money even when the market is declining.

By the time you finish this book you are going to have a complete understanding of what it means to trade options and how you can using options trading to earn extra money. You will understand several different strategies that you can use in options trading and you will understand what the risks are with each strategy. You will also know exactly what your next step should be if you are interested in earning extra money from trading options.

Thanks again for downloading this book, I hope you enjoy it!

Chapter 1-What is Options

Before you can begin trading options and stocks you need to understand what you are trading or purchasing. Of course we all know what stocks are a representation of the assets of a company after the discharge of all debt. Stocks are usually broken down into shares which will represent a fraction of ownership of a company.

An option is an agreement between a buyer and seller where they agree upon selling and purchasing an asset usually a stock at some future date. As the name suggest this sale is optional, this means that the buyer is not obligated to purchase the asset from the seller on the agreed upon date but if the buyer does choose to purchase the asset the seller is required to sell the asset, it does not matter if the value of the asset has increased or decreased.

The best way to understand options is to look at it in a common scenario. Let's imagine that you want to purchase a house but you will not have the money for another six months. The will seller agree that if you will pay an extra one percent on the house he will hold it for you for those six months. Once the six months is over you have the option to buy the house or to not buy the house. If you choose to purchase the house, the buyer is obligated to sell it to you as long as you pay the extra one percent. If however you have found that the value of the house has dropped and it would not benefit you to purchase the house you do not have to buy it, the contract is voided and the seller is allowed to sell the house to another buyer.

This type of option would be called a call option which is when a buyer has the option of purchasing an asset on an agreed upon date. There is also another type of option which is called a put option. A put option is when a buyer is allowed to purchase an asset and then immediately sell it to another party, in the United States the put option can be exercised before the agreed upon date of the call option if both the buyer and the seller agree.

This mean that if you were going to purchase a home and you and the seller agreed that you would pay for the home in six months, as long as the seller agrees, you can sell the house to a third party before the six months is over.

Of course there are advantages as well as disadvantages to option trading. One is that the buyer takes the risk of paying a fee for an option and the trade never happens. This means that if you were going to purchase a house and agreed that you would pay cash for the house in six months and the seller agreed with you but wanted a one percent interest fee each month, even though you paid the fee maybe you decided that for some reason you did not want to purchase the house on the agreed upon date, you would still be out the money you paid the seller.

Option trading does however usually benefit the buyer more than it does the seller but you also need to determine if a third party will be involved in the trade. In some trades you will have to involve a third party for instance a broker and when this third party is involved you will have to consider their fees as well.

Option trading can have its advantages as well, one such advantage is that the buyer will be able to hold on to their money a little bit longer which will allow them to earn extra interest on the money, it can also allow them to ensure that they are going to make a profit when they are considering purchasing a stock or asset that they fill is risky.

Now that you know basically how options trading works let's look at an example of options trading when it comes to stocks. Let's imagine that you want to buy a stock in Wal-Mart at some point in the future but you are worried you will lose money. Currently the stock price is 125 dollars per share and the company is doing well at the moment and the price may go up so you decide to do a call option which will allow you to have the option of purchasing 10 shares at 125 dollars in 60 days.

Once you have the option all you have to do is wait. Once the 60 days is up you realize that the stocks rose to 230 dollars per share. You now have the option to purchase 10 shares at 125 dollars each, this would provide you with an amazing profit and there would be no reason for you to not use your option and purchase the shares. Now let's say that instead of the stocks rising you find out that the price dropped to 80 dollars per share, you would end up losing money if you decided to use your option and purchase the shares so at this time you would simply let the option contract expire and purchase the stock for 80 dollars per share instead.

Many people think that there is more to options trading than this but the fact is that this really is all there is to it. Many people also are afraid to try options trading because they think that it is something that they would not be able to understand. This means that they are not taking advantage of all of the ways that they can make money in the stock market and are missing out on adding options trading to their portfolio.

Options trading allows you to have a large pay out when you decide to sell your shares. Let's go back and take a look at the Wal-Mart scenario. If you purchased the stock at 125 dollars when the price rose to 230 dollars and you were afraid to hold on to the stock due to fear of the price dropping, you would be able to sell it right then and make a profit of 1,050 dollars. It really is that easy.

Before we go any further, I do want to make sure that you understand that options trading is not a get rich quick scheme and anyone who tells you that they got rich over night by trading options is doing nothing more than lying to you. Options trading does take work and you will have to educate yourself. There will be times when you do not make a huge profit and there will be times when you come out with a large profit but no one gets rich overnight and they do not get rich without doing the work.

The difficulty of options trading can very, there are times when it will seem very easy and there are times when it will become very difficult.

Brokers will warn you that options trading is not for everyone but you do not have to worry about lack of knowledge when it comes to options trading because you have the ability to obtain the knowledge that you need. It is my hope that by reading this book you will feel more comfortable taking part in options trading and you will be able to not only expand your portfolio but you will be able to learn how to profit from options trading.

Chapter 2- Why Trade Options

Why should you trade options? This is one of the easiest but also one of the most important questions that you can ask when you are considering trading options.

The first thing that you need to understand is that options trading has seen a huge increase in popularity in the United States in recent years and it is believed that in future trades, option trading will be more common than single stock trading. There are four main reasons as to why options trading has become so popular and will continue to gain popularity and they are leverage, flexibility, low capital requirement, and rewards, smart calculation.

In this chapter I want to go over the main reasons as to why options trading has become so popular so that you can understand why you should consider trading options.

The first reason is leverage and it is the number one reason for trade options becoming so popular over recent years. What this means is that the buyer is able to make a larger profit with less risk. Remember when we talked about the Wal-Mart stocks? The buyer would have been able to purchase 10 stocks for 1250 dollars and could have sold them immediately for 2300 dollars. This ensures that the buyer has very little risk and that they are able to earn a profit on their stocks.

It also means that if that same stock had a temporary pull back that the buyer would not have been affected because options only close upon expiration. So unlike futures where profits and losses are measured daily, when you take advantage of options you would not lose money due to a temporary pull back.

Let's take a look at futures really quickly so you can understand the difference. Imagine that the same scenario is taking place, you want to use futures to purchase Wal-Mart stock at 125 dollars per share and the stock has a temporary pull back, and this pull back wipes out your account, you will lose your position even if the stock rebounds. Now there is money to be made with futures but there is money to be lost with futures as well. When you use options trading you take that lose out of the picture and give yourself a little bit more LEVERAGE to earn a profit.

The second reason that options has become so popular recently is that it allows flexibility. There are so many ways to ensure that your options fit your needs and help you with what you want to achieve. There are literally thousands of options strategies that you can use to ensure that you are able to make a profit. Of course I will not be detailing all of these strategies but I will discuss how to ensure that you are making a profit with options trading later on in the book.

The third reason that options trading has become so popular is that it has a low capital requirement. This is one of the main reasons why people choose to use options trading. You can trade options as long as you can pay for one options contract. The price of these contracts can run from just 10 or 20 dollars all the way up to tens of thousands of dollars.

You see when you decide to use futures you usually have to pay 25 percent upfront. Whereas with options trading contract you have to pay about 1/4th of that up front. This makes it much easier for you to ensure that you do not pay more for your stock that you want to and ensure that you are able to make a profit.

Finally rewards, smart calculation is the last reason I want to discuss. What this means is that since options are very flexible, and can easily be adjusting using various combinations and strategies, options becomes an instrument that rewards smart calculations. You can also project your profits using a butterfly spread and options appeal to those who are more tech savvy.

With all of that said, why should you choose options trading? The main reason for you to use options trading is that if a stock does not move in the direction that you are expecting you will lose much less money than if you had bought the stock outright.

Think about the Wal-Mart stocks, let's say that you have to pay 60 dollars up front for your options trading contract for 100 Wal-Mart stock. If you had purchased the stock outright it would have cost you 12,500 dollars. Now the stock price drops to 80 dollars per share and you decide that you are not going to continue with the options trading contract. You have lost 60 dollars. But had you purchased the shares you would have lost 4500 dollars. So not only does this ensure that you kept your 12,500 dollars in the bank and earned interest on the money, you did not lose 4500 dollars. It is almost a safety net for traders!

Of course I think that you should trade options but I want to make it clear that I do not think trading options should be the only thing that you do when it comes to the stock market. This is just one way to make money with stocks and it has to be used properly to ensure that you make a profit. I do not suggest that you should invest all of your money in options trading because we all know that the more diversity we have the higher the chances we have at earning a profit.

Now as wonderful as the above scenario looks, you need to understand that option trading does not come without risk and you should only invest your risk capital. This is the reason that many people suggest that you forgo options trading and invest your money in other areas but being ignorant of any type of investment will place you at a disadvantage.

Chapter 3- What You Need To Know

If you are going to do option trading there are a few things that you need to know. To start out this chapter I want to go over some of the lingo that you need to understand when it comes to options trading.

Strike price- the price at which the stock can be purchased or sold. This is the price that the stock must go above or below for a profit to be made and it must occur before the expiration date.

Listed option- this is an option that is listed on a national options exchange, it will have a fixed strike price as well as an expiration date, and each listed option represents 100 share of the company stock. This list is known as a contact.

In the money- This is when the share price is above the strike price in a call option and when the share price is below the strike price in a put option. The amount of which the share price is above or below the strike price or in the money is called the intrinsic value.

Premium- is the total cost or price of the option. We are not going to focus on the premium because it is beyond the scope of this book but involves the stock price, the strike price, the time value which is the time remaining until the contract expires as well as the instability of the stock.

Now let's dig a little deeper into an options trade we will use a fictional company called ABC Finance.

On June 1st we are going to say that ABC Finance stock price is 67 dollars and the premium or total cost is 3.15 for an August 70 call. This means that the total cost of the contract will be 315 dollars because as we have just learned a contract is 100 shares and 3.15 X 100= 315. You would of course have to add commissions to this price but for now we are going to focus only on the trade and not worry about commissions.

The strike price is 70 dollars and you can tell this because the option is an August 70 call. The number after the month will tell you the strike price. It will also tell you that the expiration date will be the third Friday of August. Since the strike price is 70 dollars this means that the stock option must rise above 70 dollars before the option is worth anything, but you also have to remember that you paid 3.15 per share so in reality the stoke has to reach 73.15 for you to break even.

Since the stock price now sits at 67 dollars and the strike price is 70 dollars the option is worthless and since you paid 315 dollars for the option you are currently down by that amount.

Now let's fast forward three weeks, the stock price is now at 78 dollars. The stock price is now 8 dollars above the strike price but you also have to deduct the amount of money you paid per stock which is 3.15. This leaves you with a profit of 4.85 per stock. Since you have 100 stock you could sell now and profit 485 dollars. Which means that you more than doubled your money in just 3 weeks.

At this point you can close your position which means that you can sell your option and walk away with your profits unless you think that the stocks are going to continue to rise. So let's imagine that you decide to let the option ride.

Upon the expiration date, the stock price sits at 62 dollars, since this is less than our strike price of 70 dollars the option is worthless and you will let it expire. You have lost your original investment of 315 dollars.

The price swing for this contract was 0 to 800 dollars, which would have allowed you to more than double your money, this is what leverage looks like in options trading.

Now you need to understand the difference of exercising and trading out. In the example above, you would have allowed your option to expire. Meaning that you held on to your option and the value was worthless even though you could have exercised the option when the stock reached a level of 78 dollars.

Statistic show that only 10 percent of options are exercised, 60 percent are traded out, and 30 percent of options expire.

As you can see there is money to be made in option trading but you can also lose money. This scenario could have taken another direction, meaning that the stock price could have continued to rise and you could have come out of the trade earning a profit but since the stock price dropped you actually lost money.

This is where knowledge of the stock market comes into play. You cannot simply jump into option trading if you have no prior experience in the market. This will ensure that you lose money because you will not understand how the market works and you will not be able to predict if the market will rise or fall.

Of course no matter how much experience you have in the market you have, you will never know for sure what the market will do but you can make an educated guess. If you have no experience in the market you will have no idea how to make a guess on the outcome.

The next thing you need to understand before you begin trading options is the types of options that exist. There are only two basic types of options, the first one is called the American option which can be at any time after purchase up until the expiration date. There is also the European option which can only be sold at the end of their lives. It should be noted that the type of option has nothing to do with where you are located.

So far we have only discussed options in the short term context but there are long term options. These options have holding times of one or more years and are usually a better option for those who are interested in a long term investment.

Long term options are called Long-term Equity Anticipation Securities or LEAPS. These LEAPS are essentially just like short term options but they provide the opportunity for the buyer to regulate and manage risk and speculate for a longer period of time.

LEAPS although not available on all stocks are available on most of the more popular stocks.

We have talked about some very simple calls and puts and these are referred to as plain vanilla options. Even though it may seem a little bit difficult to understand the subject of options at first, plain vanilla options are the easiest to understand.

Because options are so versatile, there are many different types and many different variations. We discussed this just a little bit earlier. Remember that there are literally thousands of variations when it comes to options. When an option is a non-standard option it is called an exotic option.

Before you consider purchasing an exotic option you should have a good grasp on regular option trading but I want to make sure this book has all of the information that you need so I will go over exotic options just a bit.

An exotic option just like a regular option works on the idea of having the right to buy an asset at some point in the future or being able to sell an asset at some point in the future. The difference is the way investors realize their profits using these options.

To put it simply, an exotic option is any option that differs from the standard calls and puts that are found on exchanges. A standard call option allows a buyer to purchase an asset on a given date for a specific price. A standard put option gives the buyer the right to sell a specific asset at a specific price on a specific date. These are plain vanilla options.

A choose option is a type of exotic option that allows the investor to decide if the option is a call or a put option during the life of the option. This means that the option may change from a call to a put and visa versa at given points during the life of the option.

A barrier option is a type of exotic option in which the pay off is dependent on whether the asset reaches or exceeds a predetermined price. This means that the buyer only has the right to purchase the option once the price reaches the agreed upon barrier. This differs from a plain vanilla option because the holder of a plain vanilla option can buy the asset at the strike price any time after the inception.

The Asian option also know as the average option is a great option for beginners because instead of having a payoff that is based upon the price at the age of maturity this option has a pay off that depends on the average price of the asset over a specified time period.

The main difference between plain vanilla options and exotic options is that plain vanilla options are found on major exchanges and exotic options are not found listed on any of the formal exchanges. This means that brokers are not as familiar with exotic options as they are with plain vanilla options.

Chapter 4- A Few Words Of Advice

Now that you are beginning to understand options trading a little bit, I want to explain to you that in no way are you going to be able to self-educate yourself and be successful at trading options. You are going to have to find a mentor, someone to teach you how to trade options on a personal level.

As much as I would love to be able to teach you everything you need to know about trading options in this book that is just impossible. Think about when you learned how to ride a bike, did you learn to ride by reading a book or by someone telling you how to do it? No, you had to get on the bike and try it for yourself. You had to practice and that is where a mentor can help you.

Of course I am going to do everything that I can to ensure you have all the information that it is possible for me to give you but I do not want you to get your hopes up and think that after you have finished this book you will be able to start trading options.

Reading about trading options is great but until you have someone mentor you in trading you will not be able to fully grasp the idea.

Think of options trading in the same way as you would think of brain surgery. You can read all the books about brain surgery all you want, you can scour the internet for information for days on end but that is not going to teach you how to perform brain surgery.

I think that most of us understand that we cannot become a good trader simply by reading about trading so I do not think this will come to you as a surpise. By reading this book I am sure that you can get the basics of trading down but you would not want someone performing brain surgery on you who only had the basics down and learned from a book now would you? In the same way, you do not want to risk your money when you only have the basics down that you learned from a book you will need hands on experience.

If you properly learn how to trade options you will learn that you can make money if the market is going up and you will be able to earn money if the market is going down. The problem that most people face is that they get into options trading for the wrong reason.

You see many people get into trading options because they think that it will help them to get rich quick. The fact is that if you are considering trading options because you want to get rich quick you are looking in the wrong place. I stated this earlier in the book but I want you to make sure that no matter what someone else may have told you options trading is difficult and it does take time to make money.

Options trading is actually best if it is used by people who are looking to create an additional income stream which would allow them to free up some of their time.

Remember, option trading can be very rewarding but it can also be very risky. The good news is that once you understand the ends and outs of options training, once you have finished this book and have spent some time with a good mentor you will never look at trading the same again.

Throughout the rest of this book we are going to go over the different option trading strategies that you can use to ensure you are protecting your profits.

Chapter 5- Options Trading Strategies

To finish this book I want to go over a few option trading strategies with you. This is not going to be a complete guide to all of the option strategies but it is going to be an overview of a few of the trading strategies that you can use when trading options.

One warning that I want to give you is that you should not worry about scouring the internet for all of the different options trading strategies. You will only overwhelm yourself instead, you should choose a few strategies to research and try out on your own. Pick one or two and then learn everything that you can learn about them. No one strategies is any better than the other, it is a matter of what works best for you and what will work best for you will be the one that you know the most about!

A married put position- This option works like an insurance plan for your stock purchases. We all understand how insurance works when we purchase it for our home or car, but what many people do not know is that you can purchase insurance to protect against loss in stocks.

Of course this is not actually called stock insurance but you will find that it works in the same way as auto or home owners insurance. This strategy is what we learned when we talked about the Wal-Mart stocks.

A married put position is basically an insurance that will ensure that you do not lose a lot of money if the stock market drops. If you purchase options using this strategy instead of losing 9,000 dollars you will only lose 200 dollars if the stock drops but will make a profit if the stock price rises. This is why it is considered a type of insurance.

When you establish a married put position it would be considered as hedging your investment in the investment community.

The protective put is essentially the same thing as a married put in that they both protect you from loss. The difference is that an investor will purchase a protective put for stock that they already own. It is considered protective because it is used by investors to protect the profits they have already made in a trade and like a married put it is used in order to protect the investor against loss when trading.

Here is an example:

Let's imagine that you purchased 100 share of ABC company at 50 dollars per share, not taking commissions into consideration this would cost you 5,000 dollars. Four months after you purchase the stock it is trading at 80 dollars per stock which will give you a 3000 dollar unrealized profit.

Normally you would have to sell your stock in order to lock in your profits but if you do this you will not be able to take advantage of future rises in that stock. Buying a protective put would solve this issue.

What you would want to do at this point is purchase a protective put with a strike price of 80 dollars. This will ensure that you do not lose your profit but just like any other type of insurance you would have to pay the premium. This option would cost you 400 dollars, so for the price of 400 dollars you are insuring your profit of 3,000 dollars.

You have therefore protected yourself against a loss. Even if the stock price drops to 50 dollars you still hold the right to sell the stock at 80 dollars up until the expiration date.

If you follow this example you will see how the put option will protect you from losing money in the market. You can also roll up your options. If the price of the stock continued to rise above the 80 dollar strike that you had on your put option you would want to consider selling that option and purchasing a new one with a higher strike price but you want to ensure that you are not doing this often or you will lose all of your profits.

One example of this is that if the price of the stock suddenly jumps from 80 to 120 dollars, the put option would not be as valuable to you so you would simply sell that option and purchase one with a strike price of 120 dollars.

You will greatly appreciate this strategy if you have a stock drop drastically on you. The great thing about this strategy is that it allows you to take advantage of potential gains while protecting yourself against potential losses. And the cost is usually low compared to the amount of money that you will be making.

I know that a lot of people will tell you that trading options is risky and it should be avoided. I know that many people do avoid trading options because they feel that it is very risky but I am hoping that by learning these two strategies you will understand that trading options does not have to be risky and there are ways for you to ensure your profit when trading options.

We have learned how buying put options can help you to hedge your investment and give you a bit of insurance but now I want to explain to you how you can use put options to help you make a profit when the stock is declining in value.

As we know, a put option has a strike price. Now let's say that your strike price is 70 dollars but the stock price has dropped to 60 dollars. Many people would say at this point that the option is worthless and let it expire but if you want to make money while the market is declining you would understand that because your strike price is 70 dollars you are able to sell this stock for 70 dollars and not for 60 dollars.

This means that you hold a contract that will allow you to sell something for more than what the market value of that asset is. This may seem a bit unfair to the buyer and it may seem a bit upside down but think of it like baseball cards.

Baseball cards are nothing more than a piece of card board but there are some that are worth very little to nothing because there are so many of them, but there are also these small pieces of card board that are worth thousands of dollars because there were not many printed and collectors desire them. Now it is a bit unfair to charge thousands of dollars for a small piece of card board but that is just the way baseball card collecting works.

In that same way, this is just how the market works. When there is a limited number of something available it makes it worth more money. Therefore even though the market has declined and your stocks are not worth 70 dollars, you hold a contract that says you can sell them for 70 dollars. Since there are not going to be a lot of these shares for sale, you will be able to ensure that you do not lose money when selling your shares by using the put option.

The amount of money you can make using this strategy depends on how far the price of the stock falls and since a stock cannot fall further than zero that will be the maximum amount of money you can earn. The good thing about this is that you do not have to worry about losing more than you invest. For example if you invest 100 dollars and the stock price rises above your strike price, the put option is worthless and you will only lose the 100 dollars you invested.

The great thing about a put option is that it allows you to take advantages of downward turns in the market and allows you to make money when others are losing money. You also only have a small risk most of the time since the only amount of money that you can lose is the amount of money you invest and this is normally a small amount.

This option also gives you leverage meaning that it allows you to use a small amount of money to make a huge profit. It also provides you with higher returns on your investment.

There are also a few disadvantages when it comes to a put option. One of the disadvantages is that a put option does have an expiration date so this means that time is working against you when you are using this strategy. The second disadvantage is that in order for you to make a profit with a put option the market has to make a downward turn. If the stock stays flat or does not make a downward turn you will lose your investment.

As you can see, there are no guarantees when it comes to the market so when people tell you that trading options is risky they are telling the truth but when you are working with the market there is going to be risk involved.

The final thing I want to discuss with you is buying call options when the market is increasing. If you buy a call option when the market is increasing you can potentially make a profit of 50 to 100 percent but of course there are always risks involved.

This strategy is one that most investors use often and it usually makes them more money than the other strategies we have discussed. If you remember from earlier chapters, a call option gives the buyer the option to purchase but does not require them to purchase. If the buyer chooses to purchase the seller is required to sell.

A call option will go up in value when the stock that it is attached to goes up in price and it will decline in value when the stock that it is attached to goes down in price. One of the great things about call options is that there is no limit on the amount of money that can be made.

This is because there is no cap on how high the value a stock can rise. This means that there is no cap on the amount that you can profit. Using call options also allows you to take advantage of upward turns in the market without having to own your own stock, since you are not purchasing the stock you risk much smaller amounts of money which also means that the most you can lose is what you pay for the Call.

Using a call option will also give you leverage which means that you are using a small investment to obtain huge gains. It also provides you with a higher potential for gain on your investments.

Of course this sounds wonderful but you have to be aware of the disadvantages of a call option as well. The first disadvantage of a call option is that they do have an expiration date so again time will work against you.

The stock also has to make an upward turn in order for you to profit. If the stock does not move or decreases in value you will lose your investment.

Call options are very simple when it comes to making a profit. Remember when we discussed purchasing an option at 60 dollars and the value raising up to 83 dollars? This is when you would make a profit with a call option. You have the option to purchase the stock at 60 dollars even though the market value is 83 dollars. This means that you can turn around and sell the shares making a profit of 23 dollars per share. Or you can purchase the stock at the low price you have locked in and hold on to it if you feel that the value will continue to increase.

Those are the basics when it comes to trading options. Of course that is not all there is to it and I do not recommend that you should jump into trading options after reading this book. What I do suggest is that you do more research, choose a strategy and learn everything you can about it and I suggest that you get a mentor. Find someone who is willing to help you when it comes to options trading. You may have to invest a bit of money at first but trust me paying someone to help you out will be worth it.

I also want to make sure that you understand that using any of the strategies discussed in this book does not mean that you are going to make a profit with the market. Trading options comes with risks and each of these strategies comes with their own risks. There is not guaranteed profit when it comes to trading options.

Conclusion

Thank you again for downloading this book!

I hope this book was able to help you to learn about options trading and how you can use it to create an additional income stream.

The next step upon successful completion of this book is to find a mentor to help you learn more about options trading. Remember that you cannot learn everything you need to know about options trading from reading a book. You must have some hands on experience.

Finally, if you enjoyed this book, please take the time to share your thoughts and post a review on Amazon. It'd be greatly appreciated!

Thank you and good luck!

www.ingramcontent.com/pod-product-compliance
Lightning Source LLC
Chambersburg PA
CBHW020956180526
45163CB00006B/2397